PRAISE FOR RITCH EICH'S
PREVIOUS BOOKS

Real Leaders Don't Boss:
Inspire, Motivate, and Earn Respect from Employees and Watch
Your Organization Soar

"Ritch Eich is a leader's leader, with a magical ability to turn the impossible into the possible. He brings to whatever he does exceptional experience, know-how, enthusiasm, and connections. Now, with his book, his unique transformational approach to leadership will be available to everyone."

—William Kearney, senior vice president, Merrill Lynch

"Ritch Eich's leadership style is part Warren Bennis and Max De Pree, part Robert Greenleaf and Peter Drucker, and part Jackie Robinson and Colin Powell. Ritch is a change agent and has worked tirelessly to transform the management practices and processes he inherited in each of his positions of increasing responsibility. As a leadership and management consultant, Ritch is continuing to share 'best practices' from the leadership field."

—Steve Grafton, president and CEO,
The University of Michigan Alumni Association

Leadership Requires Extra Innings:
Lessons on Leading from a Life in the Trenches

"Ritch Eich does a masterful job of sharing his wisdom and lifelong leadership insights. The book is an instant classic."
—Noel M. Tichy, bestselling author of *The Leadership Engine: How Winning Companies Build Leaders at Every Level*

"You always look to Ritch Eich's next volume on leadership with anticipation that he'll shake up the lineup when it comes to conventional thinking but this one gives us more. If the need for inspirational thinking for leaders is going extra innings, then Ritch is our 'closer' and ready to bring the argument home."
—Mike McCurry, former White House Press Secretary for President Clinton; Principal, Public Strategies Washington, Inc.; Director/Professor, Center for Public Theology, Wesley Theological Seminary

Truth, Trust + Tenacity:
How Ordinary People Become Extraordinary Leaders

"From one of today's most respected leaders—a priceless collection of insights that will excite and challenge the reader. I heartily recommend this book to anyone wishing to understand leadership in a meaningful way."
—Marshall Goldsmith, *New York Times* bestselling author of *What Got You Here Won't Get You There*

"This third volume is leadership expert Ritch Eich's most important book yet!"

—Ora Hirsch Pescovitz, M.D., nationally-recognized pediatric endocrinologist and researcher, former CEO, University of Michigan Health System; former CEO, Riley Hospital for Children; President, Oakland University

Leadership CPR:
Resuscitating the Workplace through Civility, Performance and Respect

"Ritch Eich has served up an *ace* with his latest book, *Leadership CPR*. His approach to writing is similar to his approach to tennis: *leave it all on the court*. As a longtime tennis coach, I greatly appreciate the preparation, attention to detail, discipline, and valuable lessons included in Ritch's *must-read* leadership book."

—Dick Gould, coach of seventeen Stanford Men's NCAA Champion teams; John L. Hinds Director of Tennis (ret.), Stanford University

"Ritch Eich defines the choices one makes on the journey to becoming a great leader. It follows my beliefs that great leadership can happen only when all actions are grounded on strong values. The book covers a lot of new ground, including leadership on boards and learning from sports and arts leaders."

—Verena Kloos, CEO, Strategic Design Consulting and former President, BMW Design Works

"*Leadership is solving problems. The day soldiers stop bringing you their problems is the day you have stopped leading them. They have either lost confidence that you can help or concluded you do not care. Either case is a failure of leadership.*"

—COLIN POWELL

LEADING WITH
GRIT,
GRACE,

GRATITUDE

Timeless Lessons for Life

Ritch K. Eich, PhD

Leading with Grit, Grace, & Gratitude

Published by RKE Books
www.ritcheichleadership.com

Editorial and project management:
Second City Publishing Services LLC
www.secondcitypublishing.com

Book Cover Design & Layout: Summer R. Morris
www.sumodesignstudio.com

Printed in the United States of America

ISBN: 978-0-578-69828-1

DEDICATION

This book is dedicated to first responders and others who demonstrated their amazing leadership skills and exceptional courage when facing a new and potentially deadly challenge during the 2020 COVID-19 pandemic. To these frontline heroes – our nurses, physicians, emergency medical personnel, hospital staff, police officers, firefighters, volunteers, public works members, paramedics, military, and many other workers whose jobs put them doubly in harm's way during the pandemic – bless you!

ACKNOWLEDGMENTS

"Too often we underestimate the power of a touch, a smile, a kind word, a listening ear, an honest compliment, or the smallest act of caring, all of which have the potential to turn a life around."—Lao Tzu

To my entire family, friends, colleagues, teachers, coaches, fellow military, clergy, mentors, editors, and publishers—thank you for being there.

DETAILS MATTER

Operation Overlord, the D-Day invasion of France during World War II, was the most critical event in the Allied effort to win the war. It *had* to succeed.

While U.S. General Dwight Eisenhower was overseeing the planning for the massive D-Day invasion, he spent an enormous amount of time hammering out what some people would consider to be mundane logistical details to ensure that the Allies had enough capable landing craft to transport troops to the Normandy beaches.

In times of great challenge or crisis, we need leaders we can trust who will take on the heavy responsibility to sweat the details.

The Minute Man by Daniel Chester French is an inspiring sculpture in Concord, Massachusetts that embodies the themes of this book. The young man who trades in his plow for a long gun symbolizes the everyday leaders among us who, in times of great need, set their own comfort and safety aside to rise up and face the challenges in front of us. Mike Goldman, a good friend and retired Indiana National Guardsman, carved this version for me from a single piece of cherry indigenous to Camp Atterbury, Indiana.

CONTENTS

PREFACE

Authors write books for many different reasons. Bob Schieffer, of CBS News and *Face the Nation* fame, revealed that when he wrote *Bob Schieffer's America* he had no lofty aspirations and would be happy "if these pieces evoke an occasional smile and perhaps cause a reader to pause here and there and say, 'I really never thought of it that way before.'"

Robert Sutton wrote *The No Asshole Rule* because he said "most of us, unfortunately, have to deal with assholes in our workplaces. ... The little book shows how to keep these jerks out of the workplace, how to reform those you're stuck with, how to expel those who can't or won't change their ways, and how to limit destruction that these demeaning creeps cause."

Caroline Kennedy edited *Profiles in Courage for Our Time*, a collection of acts of valor by writers of distinction. As she said,

"My father believed in the power of words to lead, to inspire, and to bring about change in the world."

Robert M. Edsel's *The Monuments Men* first grabbed our attention when he said "most of us are aware that World War II was the most destructive war in history…but what if I told you there was a major story about World War II that hasn't been told, a significant story at the heart of the entire war effort, involving the most unlikely group of heroes you've never heard of?"

Never Dull, a treasure trove of captivating sports and special interest stories by my wonderful friend and former *Boston Globe* sportswriter, editor, and mentor extraordinaire, Larry Ames, is a book that advances our understanding of the human condition.

My own book is organized around three simple, yet essential, values of leadership that are often overlooked: grit, grace, and gratitude. Each chapter describes people, organizations, and events that have demonstrated:

> *Grit* by transforming their organizations through bold, innovative, and sometimes controversial major change initiatives.

> *Grace* when serving others magnanimously, frequently in unexpected ways and often under fire.

> *Gratitude* by understanding what it means to treat others well, and never forgetting that others depend on you.

My sincere hope for *Leading with Grit, Grace, and Gratitude: Timeless Lessons for Life* is simple: that it is used as a reminder of the importance of having a positive outlook even in the worst of times; that it be an easy-to-read, practical book so you can go back to it from time to time as a refresher; and that for especially younger and aspiring leaders that you never forget that you can do practically anything you set your mind on. Enjoy!

GRIT

"Those who fail to learn from history are condemned to repeat it."

—WINSTON CHURCHILL

CHAPTER 1

LEARN FROM THE PAST, EMBRACE THE FUTURE

If you had told me four decades ago that my career path would include being asked to join the board of directors of my alma mater's half-million, living-member alumni association; that I would become the chair of our regional for-profit hospital's board of trustees; or that I would publish five books on leadership, I would have likely laughed out loud. But then again, I've always believed what my parents said about God working in "mysterious ways."

In retrospect, I think my curiosity with leadership can be traced back to being selected for the Marysville (CA) Little League "All-Star" team to play first base. The team's manager, Ralph Leslie Palm, was someone I greatly admired. He was a highly decorated WWII veteran with a calm, steady, and nurturing exterior backed up by an intensively competitive interior drive. It was a leadership approach that brought out the best every player had to offer.

Such leadership wisdom is not always appreciated in the moment, and it is only in retrospect that the lessons of my childhood postseason baseball coach are clear to me. As a healthcare and higher education executive since my early thirties, I have reported principally to either the CEO or president. Part of my responsibilities in these jobs was to have my boss' back, by ensuring that he or she didn't make inadvertent mistakes that might damage the reputation of the organization.

As my leadership responsibilities grew, I made sure to develop an informal cadre of trusted advisers from widely divergent careers whose candor, good judgment, and street-savvy I could count on when needed. Such a "community" advisory approach is what former Eli Lilly and Company senior executive and current Oakland University President Ora Hirsch Pescovitz, M.D., calls "a mentor's quilt." It's an approach that the University of Michigan and some U.S. presidents have chosen to embrace when they reach out to retired executive officers or cabinet officers for limited duration special assignments.

One of the best pieces of advice I received from all of my mentors was to embrace the future and welcome change. Certainly, we can—and should—learn from past mistakes, but we should not become weighed down by them. Change is inevitable, so why not face it head-on. Leaders who focus on the past—the "what ifs" scenarios of what might have been—will find themselves frustrated, and unable to lead.

The often-quoted Boy Scout motto, "Be Prepared!" served me well when I was a Boy Scout and it continues to serve me well today; this is a particularly important leadership standard given today's corporate environment and the rapid, breathtaking rate of change. As someone who has helped guide three major organizational change initiatives, I can attest to the importance of keeping this age-old trope in mind. Here are three suggestions to consider that have helped me move forward:

1. Thoroughly scan your organization's landscape and identify all the ways an initiative could be scuttled. As one of my former bosses advised me: first, find the unexploded, hidden landmines, then identify the potential "rogue actors" and develop a written plan to deal with these threats. Keep your eye on these threats throughout the process and never underestimate the potential resistance to even a well-laid plan. Don't be surprised by comments like: "We've done this before, and it didn't work then."

2. Embed the initiative in the organization and engage the *entire* workforce in the effort. Ensure that everyone involved has a voice and is consulted and supported along the way, even when the views offered are negative and skeptical of the plan. Failure to encourage expressions of skepticism, criticism, and opposing ideas quickly erodes any trust previously garnered in the process. In my first book, *Real Leaders Don't Boss,* I described how former Indianapolis 500 "Rookie of the Year" race driver and current Chelsea Milling Company ("JIFFY" Mix) President and CEO Howdy Holmes used some of these techniques to bring about major change for sustained superior performance that continues today.

3. Ensure that the CEO and his or her executive team understand the key idea that no single department (e.g., the marketing department) owns the change initiative and the implementation plan. Change must be an integral part of everyone's role and responsibility, including upper management and the managers who report to them. I was hired by an organization whose governing board mandated the desired change with less than full buy-in from the executive team, whose interest and commitment varied considerably. As a result, the

initiative was an uphill challenge from the start without this essential and consistent support. Remember, change isn't an abstract, academic event; it's highly personal and emotions often run high. Inspired leadership never stops working to ensure that honest sharing of contrary views in a trusting environment is an essential element for organizational buy-in. And this is critical at every level of the organization—don't expect line workers to embrace change because you said they should. Make sure they are a part of the initiative so they feel ownership.

The 2017 Academy Awards Best Picture nominee *Hidden Figures* is a movie about three brilliant and inspiring female black NASA employees in the 1960s who used their intelligence and dogged determination to succeed, despite an atmosphere of degrading racism and sexism. The trio, programmer Dorothy Vaughn, math genius Katherine Johnson, and engineer Mary Jackson, played a crucial role in America's efforts to put astronaut John Glenn in space and best our Soviet nemesis. This film reminds us how difficult change can be in any organization, especially when years of traditions, habits, and behavioral norms stand in the way. In 1941, one of my favorite heroines, First Lady Eleanor Roosevelt, a woman of great conviction and a tireless devotee for civil rights for African Americans, visited

Alabama's Tuskegee Institute during a period when much of our nation was highly skeptical of African Americans' intelligence and aptitude. During her tour she mentioned that she had been told by many that black people couldn't fly, and she asked C. Alfred Anderson, a black flight instructor, if he'd take her up! To the horror of her staff and Secret Service protection, he said yes, so the First Lady strapped herself into the back seat of a plane and flew with the sole black flight instructor who had a commercial pilot's license. This same pilot would later train the famed Tuskegee Airmen.

The wisest leaders are not just smart; they often have an uncanny ability to not only embrace the future, but to see it as well. I reported to the CEO of a large hospital for several years; he seemed to have an ability to "see around the corner." It is this type of ability that allows these leaders to move quickly to seize a market advantage. Columnist Tom Friedman believes that we, as a species, are standing at a moral intersection and today's leaders have two pathways to follow. One begins the process of fixing everything (world poverty, terrorism, climate change— the big bucket things). Another path leads to the end of our species. Leaders must get ahead of these monumental challenges with values-driven leadership that moves us to a far better, more sustainable future.

A hallmark of the "JIFFY" Mix success story is Howdy Holmes' firm belief in the necessity of making long-term decisions. Emphasizing sustained competitive advantage is not a new concept for Holmes. Previously, he was a successful motor sports company executive, author, and one of the first color commentators on racing for ESPN. But, it was a distinct shift in culture for the company when Holmes assumed the reins of Chelsea Milling thirty-three years ago. As he readily admits, Holmes had to redesign his own "personal delivery system" when he assumed the helm of the 132-year-old family-owned business. And, imagine the changes his grandfather had to make beginning in 1930 when his grandmother, Mabel White Holmes, created the first corn muffin mix in America. Howdy quickly learned that to be successful in transforming this packaged food company, his car racing experience didn't matter and he had to reinvent himself. And, so he did, and part of the company's renaissance was Holmes' strong commitment to personal growth for everyone in the firm, from hourly to salaried workers. Two years ago he put in place a final pillar of the company's reorganization by hiring a personal development director. Among the director's many duties is giving every employee who wants to learn and grow new opportunities to expand their duties at work. Building on but expanding well beyond the firm's historical and strong employee-centered philosophy, the director implemented talent assessments, career progression, training opportunities, organizational evaluations, team building interventions, and competency models for his workers. Howdy saw the future and embraced it.

In *Moneyball*, the 2011 baseball movie that was nominated for six Oscars, Oakland A's general manager Billy Beane hires a Yale-educated data analyst to evaluate players' potential using a nontraditional, statistics-driven set of criteria. The A's scouts and manager were outraged by the introduction of the new methodology, but eventually the innovative analytic technique was used to create a successful team, one that could operate on the league's smallest payroll. Billy Beane wrote a new chapter in a very tradition-driven sport. Your goal as a leader should be to chart an innovative, forward-thinking path for your organization.

Ben Ferencz is the last living prosecutor from the Nuremberg Trials that tried Nazi war criminals at the end of WWII. Leslie Stahl interviewed him in 2019 for *60 Minutes*. Despite his traumatic experience, Ferencz remains both an optimist and a realist when assessing the future. In fact, he's supporting this optimistic future by dedicating his life savings to the Genocide Prevention Institute at the U.S. Holocaust Memorial Museum.

His message to the rest of us when the current state of affairs in our world discourages us: "It takes courage not to be discouraged." I would add to that: It takes courage to embrace the future with enthusiasm!

"If we are to achieve a richer culture, rich in contrasting
values, we must recognize the whole gamut of human
potentialities, and so weave a less arbitrary social fabric, one in
which each diverse human gift will find a fitting place."

—MARGARET MEAD

CHAPTER 2

CELEBRATE DIFFERENCES, DON'T DENOUNCE THEM

My career working with leaders in industry and the armed services has given me a unique opportunity to help advance opportunities for women, as well as minorities. There are several lessons I learned—from both male and female leaders—that can be applied to improving diversity in the workplace. If you think about it, why wouldn't you want your organization, especially your board, more representative of the population at large (i.e., your customer base)?

When it comes to women, the reality among too many people is that a woman's primary goal in life is raising a family—everything else is secondary.

Besides the obvious observation that women should be proportionately represented, women can be more effective leaders because they are often more conciliatory and less dogmatic than their male counterparts when it comes to decision-making. They view compromising as a sign of confidence and strength—this strength is sorely lacking in many organizations, and on many boards.

When women are at the table, organizations almost always experience more success: better ideas surface, more viable policy alternatives are created, the quality of the discussion is heightened, and financial returns are stronger. The reason isn't necessarily because there are women present as much as the organization is no longer an "old boys club."

Diversity can give organizations a competitive edge— imagine the Dodgers without Jackie Robinson or the Tigers without Hank Greenberg.

In 1947, legendary Brooklyn Dodgers General Manager Branch Rickey's bold leadership brought Jackie Robinson, an African American—and my childhood hero—to the major leagues. One of the first players to embrace Robinson was Hank Greenberg, a future Hall of Famer himself who, by the time Robinson broke the color barrier, was playing for the Pittsburgh Pirates. As a Jew, Greenberg had endured extensive anti-Semitic verbal abuse and death threats throughout his career so he knew firsthand the persecution and hatred Robinson would face. Greenberg advised Robinson that the best way to achieve victory was to beat his critics on the field.

Robinson was a natural leader who understood the importance of working with others, being true to yourself, and balancing personal and professional commitments. More than seventy years after his groundbreaking accomplishment, the odds Robinson faced and the obstacles he overcame can teach us why it's so important to focus on results instead of someone's ethnic makeup or gender.

While racism and bigotry still exist today, it was worse in the United States of the 1940s. Robinson overcame the odds by focusing on results—scoring and winning games. With the exception of teammate Pee Wee Reese, very few welcomed him as an equal when he joined the Dodgers, but he still succeeded because his fellow players couldn't argue with success.

Despite Jackie Robinson's incredible athletic ability and his spiritual upbringing, it is unlikely that he could have weathered the years of racial taunts, death threats, and opponents' numerous intentional attempts to hurt him and end his baseball career without his wife, Rachel. At one point, when talking about himself, Jackie stopped using the pronoun "I" instead using "we" as in Rachel and me. The bond they shared could not be broken. It is important to note that the Jackie Robinson story is rightfully also the story of Rachel Isum, his equal!

Those who bear the burden of overcoming bias, racism, or sexism in the business world due to their ethnicity, skin color, or gender deserve the opportunity to compete on a level playing field. A diverse workforce will help create a more just, vibrant, and successful workplace.

Diversity enhances a company's reputation and public image. Diverse businesses attract top talent and more customers from all groups. Consider this: nationwide, minorities command almost $4 trillion in annual purchasing power, according to the Selig Center for Economic Growth at the University of Georgia, which also found that minority consumer markets have grown faster than the buying power of white people since 2000. According to Linda Landers at Girlpower Marketing, women command $7 trillion and make 85 percent of all consumer purchasing decisions.

A person's gender, race, and ethnic background help shape their worldview and experience. It's common sense that a wise corporate strategy would accept and welcome diversification into both the workplace and the boardroom, and that companies would want their workforce to mirror their diverse customer base.

Some companies have already figured this out. One is Salesforce Inc., a software company based in San Francisco that has consistently appeared in the top 10 on Fortune's list of the 100 Best Companies to Work For. Salesforce's founder, chairman, and CEO, Marc Benioff, is among those who signed the CEO Action for Diversity & Inclusion Pledge, an initiative launched by a group of business leaders in June 2017 that bills itself as "the largest CEO-driven business commitment to advance diversity and inclusion in the workplace," according to its webpage, with over 500 CEOs signing on. The pledge includes a promise to encourage dialogue about inclusivity and diversity in the workplace, create accountability systems, and implement and expand unconscious bias education, among other actions.

The companies and CEOs taking the pledge also promise to share resources and what they've learned—yet another best practice to spread not only the *why*, but the *how* a business improved inclusiveness and how other businesses can too.

There are lots of reasons to want a diverse workforce and board, including the following:

1. *Promote innovation, curiosity, and creativity:* Bold, new ideas happen as people of different perspectives, life circumstances, and cultures intermingle. According to the University of San Francisco's *Guide to Managing Diversity in the Workplace*, "Heterogeneity promotes creativity and heterogeneous groups have been shown to produce better solutions to problems and a higher level of critical analysis." Women and minorities offer new

perspectives and new ideas based on their life experiences and help a company outthink the competition, while homogenous groups of workers often repeat the same ideas—and the same mistakes.

2. *Customer loyalty requires diversity:* A diverse employee base in marketing, sales, product design, and other departments is important. Customers are often leery of interacting with companies whose employees are of one background, one color, and one mind-set. As stated above, research shows that women make most of the consumer purchasing decisions (including for their families), so if your company makes and sells cars, houses, or any household product, women should be among those to design and sell them. Diversity provides keen insight into the customer base and mirrors customer desires.

3. *Expand your talent pool:* Boards of directors, senior management, middle management, and front-line employees must be diverse if the applicant pool is going to find your business attractive. As Maureen Crawford Hentz, Vice President of Human Resources at A.W. Chesterton, explains in her article "Managing Millennials," younger workers "have been raised,

schooled and socialized in environments decidedly more multicultural than other generations. For many Millennials, diversity is a given: women have always been equal and multilingualism is a norm." Several other studies show that minority applicants avoid businesses they view as not diverse. Job seekers want to work with companies with a diverse workforce, that don't discriminate in hiring, and have an open and inclusive environment. As for women, they offer an educational advantage over male applicants: women now earn the majority of bachelor's degrees, master's degrees, and advanced degrees like PhDs, medical degrees, and law degrees in the United States, according to the National Center for Education Statistics.

4. *Changing demographics force the issue*: As we rapidly approach the point in time when minorities represent the majority of new job applicants, businesses will compete for a shrinking percentage of available talent. There simply won't be enough white males to hire. Considering the current population growth rates, the population of minorities will probably surpass America's non-Hispanic white population by 2050, and in several parts of our nation, many years before then. As of July

2019, women comprised 50.8 percent of the United States population, according to estimates from the U.S. Census Bureau. Non-Hispanic whites comprised about 60 percent of the population in 2019 compared to 75 percent in 1990. Minorities and mixed race people now comprise about 40 percent of the population nationwide, and foreign-born people comprise 13.4 percent, according to Census estimates. White males continue to be a declining percentage of the overall population.

With women and minorities increasing in number, purchasing power, and clout, a smart, forward-thinking organization will want to take advantage of the benefits a diverse workforce delivers. Besides that, it is the right practice to follow—a position I've taken for several decades.

"To me, ideas are worth nothing unless executed. They are just a multiplier. Execution is worth millions."

—STEVE JOBS

CHAPTER 3

Sweat the Details

As a young enlisted sailor, I was taught how to salute and march properly, perform my duties to the best of my ability, work as a team, and wear my dress blues and summer whites smartly. Later, as a naval officer, I was reminded regularly that details matter, and can be the difference between life and death. It should be no different in business—business leaders need to learn early to "sweat the details." Details matter and can be the difference between executing successfully and failure.

From my more than four decades in both the for-profit and nonprofit sectors, it has been my experience that the reasons for most *failed* executions are one or more of the following:

1. The chief executive doesn't view execution as one of his or her primary roles—he or she believes that

it is someone else's job. As a result, no one else takes execution seriously and it fails. Implementation of core strategies has to start at the top—it cannot simply be delegated (see number 2).

2. The executive team is content to delegate execution to others in the organization, essentially isolating themselves from the day-to-day challenges that can impede success. Executives often avoid those directly involved in implementation because they consider their principal responsibility to be strategy, not execution. This behavior sends the wrong message and will lead to an unsuccessful execution (see number 1).

3. Meetings are painfully and unnecessarily long, with those in charge often too deliberative or indecisive. Valuable time is wasted discussing mundane and pointless subjects that don't impact the overall success of the project. Instead of actively participating, attendees end up checking their phones or daydreaming—and execution suffers as a result.

4. The use of specific, easily understood metrics are rarely used in evaluating initiatives. If metrics are used, they drive the wrong behaviors. For example, focusing on

sales figures instead of profitability can mask production or other problems.

5. Performance reviews become routine instead of being used to improve performance and reward truly exceptional execution. Too often the wrong people are kept in the wrong jobs, compounding problems. How many times have you seen the wrong person in the wrong position because it's easier to keep the status quo?

Execution is a competence that needs to be embedded in the culture of the organization. It is a major responsibility for which the chief executive must be held accountable by the board of directors and shareholders. As investors continue to actively involve themselves in corporate governance, they will expect successful execution instead of excessive excuses.

Former University of Michigan football coach Bo Schembechler learned the importance of execution from a master practitioner, Ohio State football coach Woody Hayes. Great friends and later fierce rivals, they engaged in the now famous "Ten Year War" where either Michigan or Ohio State won the Big Ten football championship (Schembechler edged Hayes 6-5-1 in their epic struggles). Many, including myself, believe that no other teams placed more emphasis on preparing to execute and then performing effectively on game day than these two storied teams. There are many lessons today's business leaders can learn from successful coaches like Schembechler and Hayes, but placing continuous emphasis on the fundamentals of execution is one of the most important.

When Schembechler coached, he was less concerned about an opponent correctly guessing which play he had just called because he was confident he had the right players in the correct positions—one of the key components of effective execution. His players knew exactly what the desired outcome was and how they were to execute because they had relentlessly practiced the play. His vision is no less important in today's hyper fast, super competitive global economy where competition is fierce and relentless. Whether it's a sports team, a locally owned business, or a Fortune 100 organization, having the right people in the right positions, with the right experience, is critical to successful execution.

During Schembechler's twenty years as Michigan's head football coach, his players won thirteen Big Ten titles and every one of his student-athletes who stayed four years in Ann Arbor left Michigan with at least one Big Ten championship ring. Each player graduated knowing what successful execution meant—in football and in life. And, just as college football teams play an up-tempo style of game today, organizations need to be prepared to execute more quickly *and* effectively.

Any true sports enthusiast today could rattle off a long list of premier coaches in high school, college, and professional sports who emphasize execution. But a name that has often been synonymous with focusing on the details for me is Herm Edwards, head coach of the Arizona State University Sun Devils football team. A former collegiate and NFL star cornerback, Edwards has made execution his mantra by encouraging his players to ask "why" when they're told to do something. He believes that, if players don't understand why it is important to execute their role in a particular way, they will be less committed as a member of the team. Edwards sees this as central to winning football games.

I often wish every new CEO could watch the Michigan Marching Band practice their routines; be on the flight deck of a navy carrier at sea during sea qualifications; watch how "JIFFY" Mix products are made and packaged; or spend an entire day at Google headquarters in Silicon Valley as I did. All of these organizations understand the critical importance of proper execution.

Successful execution also includes an understanding—and mastering of—some essential principles of leadership. Most of these principles involve common sense, and all have a direct impact on execution:

- *Take care of your team.* Have conviction in your team and let them shine but also be prepared to accept responsibility when things don't go as planned. Never blame others but instead help resolve problems and move on—your team wants to know they can take risks but that you'll have their backs if they fall. Respect employees as individuals, and always remember that you have to continuously earn that respect from those around you. If your team knows you support them, they'll go to bat for you.

- *Never be afraid to compromise, and always be civil.* There are people who think that if you compromise, you are weak. In fact, being able to compromise is a sign of strength and confidence. Leaders who compromise come across as caring, mature leaders who are able to put others before themselves and go out of their way to spend time understanding a differing point of view, even if they don't act on it. Adopt a "zero tolerance" rule for rudeness, bullying, backbiting, and discrimination—and enforce it by terminating those who violate the rule.

Along with an inability to compromise, few actions impede a successful execution faster than incivility.

- *Avoid self-promotion and publicity stunts.* Boasting and bragging are obnoxious behaviors and can damage your reputation. There's nothing wrong with wanting to stand out and be noticed—but be sure it's sincere. Get ahead by being tenacious, trustful, and truthful—not by being disingenuous, deceitful, or dishonest. Nothing demotivates a team trying to focus on executing like a show-off.

- *Subjugate your career to the success of your team.* If your team understands that you are putting their success before your own, they'll respect your integrity and most likely perform at an even higher level. A successful execution isn't a solo event—it depends on your entire team.

Karl Weick, distinguished emeritus professor of organizational behavior at the Ross School of Business at the University of Michigan, had it right when he urged leaders facing their most pressing, ambiguous challenges to get people moving, identifying the clues, gathering ideas from all quarters, and using trial and error to make sense of the vexatious problem confronting them.

Not only does proper execution improve performance (both human and bottom line), it also leads to more insight regarding your competition. CEOs (whose tenure at any one company is generally an average of just five years) as well as other leaders would do well to remember that sweating the details is critical to their organization's success.

"If you read enough biography and history, you learn how people have dealt successfully or unsuccessfully with similar situations or patterns in the past. It doesn't give you a template of answers, but it does help you refine the questions you have to ask yourself.".."

—JAMES MATTIS

CHAPTER 4

IT TAKES AN ARMY
TO WIN A WAR

Most of what we read about the reasons for hiring veterans is written by people who never served in the military, and while well-meaning, they can often come across as patronizing:

- The unemployment rate of veterans is too high, so let's give them a job.

- They care for others, so let's care for them.

- We owe them our gratitude, so let's "thank them for their service."

In fact, the most compelling reason is simple: veterans are often the best-qualified candidates. Period. While they may not have worked in a traditional office, or have an MBA, they do have strong leadership skills, understand how to work with diverse groups, work well under pressure, know how to solve problems, and appreciate what it really takes to work as part of a team. Veterans have been taught to win—often against overwhelming odds—because their lives (and the lives of others) depend on it. Veterans bring true real-world experience to the workplace.

There's a great deal about leadership that can be learned from the armed forces, and the veterans that served.

Unfortunately, some people have preconceived notions against veterans: that they are inflexible, warmongers, and narrow in thought. According to the Defense Data Manpower Center, just .5 percent of the American population serve in the armed forces, so it's no surprise that we often misjudge and discount the contributions veterans can make. Just like other minority groups, they are often misjudged, mischaracterized, and stereotyped.

From my experience serving in leadership roles in four different industries and as both an enlisted sailor and a naval officer, I have found that most newly minted MBAs or even those with a few years' experience lack the real-world awareness and analytical skills that veterans possess.

Most veterans are ready to hit the ground running when they join an organization. They know how to lead and understand that it's also necessary to follow. Military officers are often expected to step up and take responsibility for their actions and behavior at a far younger age than those who enter the business world directly out of college—those same Marines, soldiers, and sailors are given active leadership roles and accountabilities far earlier as well. Through their experiences, they learn what authentic leadership means, including courage, a skill that is less obvious in the business world, but should be.

It takes courage to steer an organization into and through uncharted territory and to compete with fiercer and stronger brands. It takes courage to do the right thing by your co-workers and the people you manage, or to win against a fierce competitor in the marketplace.

It takes courage to try a new strategy or introduce a new product.

If organizations want sophisticated, quantitative, analytical, logistical, and operational skills—and want people who can handle all of that under pressure—take advantage of veterans.

Veterans have demonstrated remarkable flexibility in critical situations, have experience overcoming practically every form of adversity, and have gained knowledge leading and motivating others. Members of the armed forces have been taught to remain calm when things get rough and use creativity to solve problems.

While there are numerous examples throughout history of how members of the armed forces practiced leadership principles that can be applied to any organization, one of the strongest is that of Elmo R. Zumwalt Jr.

United States Navy Admiral Elmo R. Zumwalt Jr., a veteran of World War II, Korea, and Vietnam, and a humanitarian in retirement, was bold, innovative, determined, and caring. He is best remembered for his transformative efforts to modernize the sea service and its culture, reduce racism and sexism, and for his lasting commitment to enlisted personnel including women and minority sailors.

Zumwalt represented a real leader. He knew how to get things done despite challenges and pushback from superiors. He was decisive, and always tried to do the right thing. Zumwalt, the youngest person to serve as chief of Naval Operations, faced a multitude of problems internal to the Navy as well as criticism from the media and Washington pundits. He battled jealousy from other military leaders and numerous chief petty officers who resisted his reform efforts. But he courageously stood his ground and pressed forward.

Many of his achievements in the Navy had little to do with fighting or war. He treated the lowest ranking sailors with dignity and respect. He made people want to re-enlist. Through his progressive directives, known as "Z-grams," Zumwalt tried to humanize the Navy and make life better for minorities and women, Navy spouses, and junior officers. He issued directives to establish ROTC programs at predominantly black colleges, boost black enrollment at the Naval Academy, and end sexist and racist policies. He created a Minority Affairs Office, and loosened up the dress code. White sailors respected and trusted him too.

Zumwalt was also a selfless and successful leader in retirement. He helped numerous charities, advocated for those exposed to Agent Orange, and founded the national bone marrow registry, which seeks to match bone marrow donors and recipients. In awarding Zumwalt the Presidential Medal of Freedom in 1998, President Bill Clinton called him "one of the greatest models of integrity and leadership and genuine humanity our nation has ever produced."

Zumwalt shows us why the armed forces is such a great resource for other organizations—as both a treasure trove of leadership lessons and an underutilized resource for the leaders of the future.

When you think about it, what other reliable source can a business tap into to recruit men and women with real-life experiences including sophisticated quantitative, analytical, logistical, and operational skills; demonstrated flexibility honed by having faced life and death situations; experience overcoming practically every form of adversity; and experience leading and motivating scores of others? No MBA program, regardless of how good it is, can provide that.

Soldiers. Sailors. Airmen. Marines. Coastguardsmen. National Guardsmen. All frequently have impressive experience in composure and clear thinking under fire, leading under the harshest of conditions, managing and supervising others, and dedication and resolve to succeed that cannot be easily replicated by others. However, too many business leaders are unprepared to fully comprehend those experiences and how they can benefit a business. Here are five ways those with military experience can help advance an organization:

1. Veterans, even those with less experience, can frequently organize, analyze, and execute desired tasks quickly, efficiently, and with scarce resources, often with little required oversight.

2. Veterans have often conceived the strategy and implemented many of the tactics similar to what city managers, mayors, or business executives do when collaboration with others is required for a successful business venture.

3. Veterans are responsible for scrutinizing the financial numbers of the assets the Armed Forces delegated to

him (or her) during deployment: equipment typically costing millions of dollars to operate and repair.

4. Many veterans have been responsible for leading contingents of Marines, soldiers, or sailors. Businesses need managers now more than ever who can bring out the most innovative ideas from their ranks to best their competition.

5. Veterans often have to deal with both ambiguity and structure. There is little question they often bring a greater maturity, self-confidence, and stronger work ethic to the business arena than recent MBA graduates without prior military experience.

In their book *Start-Up Nation*, authors Dan Senor and Saul Singer report that "the capacity of U.S. corporate recruiters to make sense of combat experience and its value in the business world is limited." Yet other nations have figured it out…and none better than Israel, where military leadership, drive, and ingenuity have played a key role in that country's producing more start-up companies than India, China, Japan, South Korea, Canada, and the United Kingdom. During a trip to Israel, I had the opportunity to speak with several current and previous members of the Israeli Defense Forces (IDF). After completion of their obligatory service, Israeli men and women have established substantial networks with other IDF folks which aids them greatly in finding excellent jobs in Israeli corporations.

In fact, Israel's leaders place a premium on military experience for business transformation. It is no wonder, as Senor and Singer wrote, "Israel boasts the highest density of start-ups in the world and has more companies listed on the NASDAQ than companies from all over Europe."

There is a great deal we can learn about leadership from the armed forces and veterans. Astute organizations recognize the advantages—and understand that veterans know what it really takes to not only win the battle, but also the war.

As this book was going to press, the recent donnybrook regarding the Navy's nuclear-powered aircraft carrier, the USS Theodore Roosevelt (CVN-71) and the rapidly expanding spread of COVID-19 among the crew of the Roosevelt, had sparked renewed and widespread concern about the state of civilian-military relations. The incident which led to the firing of the distinguished and popular commanding officer of the carrier, Captain Brett Crozier, and the subsequent resignation of the acting Secretary of the Navy, Thomas Modley, is but the latest in an increasing number of events politicizing the military. One can only wonder if the late Admiral Elmo Zumwalt was still Chief of Naval Operations or General James Mattis, USMC (ret.) was still the Secretary of Defense, would this situation have even occurred. I'm reminded of a quotation from the ship's namesake, President Theodore Roosevelt: "The best executive is the one who has sense enough to pick good men to do what he wants done, and self-restraint enough to keep from meddling with them while they do it."

"Be a teacher. Rank does not confer privilege or give power. It imposes responsibility."

—PETER DRUCKER

CHAPTER 5

KEEP YOUR EYES ON
THE ROAD AHEAD

Concern about the direction of America has become the leadership challenge of our era. A Pew Research Center survey, released in 2019, asked Americans how they foresaw the United States in 2050. Pessimism reigned as people predicted that healthcare would be harder to afford, senior citizens would struggle to survive, the economy would weaken, income inequality would increase, and the state of the environment would deteriorate. Most respondents expressed little confidence that today's leaders could find solutions.

In times like this, it's important to look for leaders who are:

- Values-driven: Guided by principles and ideals;

- Honest: Driven by truth and ethics;

- Empathic: Care about customers and employees, not just profits;

- Respectful: Seek to strengthen the institutions that make America strong;

- Future-oriented: Plan for tomorrow, instead of only focusing on today.

These are the attributes—the basics if you will—that make up a true leader.

Unfortunately, models of true leadership can be hard to find in a sea of self-interested individuals motivated by gaining and retaining position and pleasing shareholders—but they do exist! Here are examples of leaders, past and present, who can serve as exemplars in these leadership-starved times:

1. As we read in an earlier chapter, Pasadena baseball legend Jackie Robinson broke the racial barrier in professional baseball with grit, grace, and gratitude. Self-control and excellence were his "weapons" as he fought a lifelong battle for civil rights and justice.

2. Journalistic pioneer Cokie Roberts believed in the power and value of a free press and was a tireless champion of empowerment for women. Roberts helped shape National Public Radio and flourished in journalism at a time when few women could.

3. Immaculée Ilibagiza, a Rwandan genocide survivor, inspires others through her talks and writings. Buoyed by her Catholic faith, Ilibagiza has, incredibly, forgiven the people who killed her parents and siblings during the Rwandan genocide and serves as a shining example of humanity and grace.

4. Ben Ferencz, the lead investigator and prosecutor of the Nuremberg Trials mentioned earlier in this book, tirelessly collected evidence against Nazis who committed war crimes during World War II. His conviction led him to fight, successfully, for an International Criminal Court to try those who commit crimes against humanity and to work for global peace.

5. Sally Ride broke down barriers for women and was a role model as a NASA astronaut who literally encouraged others to reach for the stars. She helped design the robot arm for the space shuttle and was the first American woman—and the youngest at the age of thirty-two—to go into space, in 1983. Her legacy to teach children about STEM lives on through Sally Ride Science, a nonprofit she co-founded.

6. Corporal Desmond T. Doss stared down death as an Army medic during World War II, saving the lives of

seventy-five men. A Seventh-day Adventist, he refused to carry a weapon when he served on the front lines. He never shirked his duty while standing firm in his convictions. He was the only conscientious objector to earn a Medal of Honor in WWII.

7. Cesar Chavez, a migrant farm worker who experienced harsh working conditions and discrimination as a child, fought for a better life for farmworkers in California and became a leading national civil rights activist through the use of nonviolent tactics and relentless persuasion.

8. Alan Mulally, former president and CEO of Ford Motor Company, displayed unfailing optimism, curiosity, and open-mindedness as he led Ford to reclaim its place as a top global automaker. Arguably one of the best CEOs in American history, Mulally thought like a designer, motivated like a coach, and built collaboration like an ambassador.

9. Finally, the students who survived the Marjory Stoneman Douglas High School shooting are an inspiration for their confidence, social media savvy, and persuasiveness, which elevated them to a leading voice in the national gun debate. They are a shining example of young people

who, like climate activist Greta Thunberg, are *demanding* solutions from resistant and myopic politicians.

Peter Drucker once said, "Effective leadership is not about making speeches or being liked; leadership is defined by results not attributes." All the leaders in this list understand the attributes of leadership—being values-driven, honest, empathic, respectful, and future-oriented. But they defined leadership through their results, from combating discrimination to expanding the conversations on gun control and climate change.

While effective leadership is defined by results, it doesn't end there. Planning for the future is critical to keep momentum moving forward.

In order to keep that momentum going, organizations must consciously and continuously strengthen their leadership pipelines and grow their pool of future leaders. Leaders need to be actively involved as advisers and counselors of younger talent at every level of their companies as mentors and expect their direct reports to do the same.

There are two immediate and pragmatic actions leaders can take to develop a leadership pipeline, and plan for the future:

1. Commit to becoming "teaching" organizations, where a conscious pledge is made to teach managers how to become leaders. The need for such resolute commitment

should be obvious: presidents, CEOs, and members of the leadership team who take time to train and guide their lieutenants ultimately experience more success in driving operating performance. Plus, employee retention is heightened while costs are lessened in organizations that effectively leverage the talent of their teams.

2. Develop a corporate culture and a leadership education structure that builds future leaders from within. For many organizations, it often seems more expedient to hire young talent from "known" entities including top academic institutions, blue-chip companies, or well-known consulting firms. While doing so often leads to short-term success, such recruiting strategies rarely deliver lasting results and true business innovation. The central spoke of a winning organization should be internally-developed leaders who understand the company's business strategy along with its culture— people who possess the internal credibility to drive insightful change and quality performance.

As acclaimed management experts Noel Tichy and Eli Cohen wrote in *The Leadership Engine*, "The job of the leader has not changed. Enhancing the value of the assets and sustaining growth are still the ultimate goals. This is accomplished by developing others to be leaders at every level and getting them aligned and energized."

The mark of a true leader is his or her ability to focus on the present (results) while simultaneously planning for the future (leadership pipeline).

GRACE

"A man wrapped up in himself makes a very small bundle."

—BENJAMIN FRANKLIN

CHAPTER 6

R-E-S-P-E-C-T:
CHECK YOUR EGO AT THE
DOOR

Meaningful leadership and an organization's culture are intertwined. A successful leader's vision, personal value system, and level of concern for the workforce become ingrained in the fabric of the corporate culture. Leadership really does start at the top.

A healthy corporate culture values the job done by each employee regardless of his or her job duties and encourages teamwork to get the job done. The best, most effective, and caring leaders realize that a positive corporate culture is the glue that connects and motivates people. It enables them to look forward to coming to work every day instead of dreading it.

The core of a positive and inclusive corporate culture often includes social responsibility and giving back to the community. It also recognizes that over-the-top CEO and executive compensation packages show greed and a lack of concern for those workers at the bottom, many who barely make ends meet. Income inequality between the C-suite and lower-wage workers needs to change for a positive corporate culture to succeed.

Successful leaders understand the impact that a strong, positive, and inclusive corporate culture has on organizational performance. These leaders treat workers—not shareholders or profits—as their greatest asset, investing in and motivating them. They expect high standards from employees that they themselves modeled and reinforced. Leaders like Microsoft's Bill Gates, one of America's most philanthropic business leaders, Yvon Chouinard of Patagonia, and Paula Ehrlich of E.O Wilson Biodiversity are all examples of leaders who, over the years, practiced the same high standards they expected from those who worked for the organizations they headed.

For most of my career, I have typically reported to the president, CEO, or chairman of the board. As a result, I've been fortunate enough to see chief executives in action in many different industries and organizations. Along the way, I have observed what the best leaders do— and learned a few lessons about what never to do:

1. Roll up your sleeves and work alongside your team. Your actions promote collaboration and cooperation, allow

you to see how your team interacts, and provide you with a great opportunity to be a mentor and coach.

2. Encourage cross-training. Cross-training allows everyone to be ready to pitch in when needed. It provides people with the opportunity to learn a new skill and can be a lifesaver in an emergency.

3. Express gratitude. After completing a project successfully, recognize everyone (and I do mean everyone) who contributed.

4. Be humble. Don't be afraid of hiring someone because you feel they might outshine you—their accomplishments will reflect well on you.

5. Be accessible. Be available to your team when they need you. You may be inconvenienced at times, but respect is reciprocal, and your accessibility demonstrates their importance to the organization.

6. Listen. Establish and promote an environment where everyone feels safe, valued, and empowered to contribute—keep an open mind and listen. Identify input that is actionable, act on it, and always give credit where it is due.

7. Recognize the little wins. Don't overlook base hits by only focusing on home runs. Singles and doubles can add up over the long term and build energy, momentum, and trust along the way.

8. Take responsibility. Don't blame others for your own mistakes. One of the surest ways to demoralize your team is to blame them for something that isn't their fault. Own up to your mistakes, focus on lessons learned, and then move on.

9. Check your ego at the door. The very best leaders are confident but not cocky—they support their teams, especially during difficult economic times.

10. Write well. It may seem passé in an era of texting but being an effective communicator means being able to write clearly, succinctly, and thoughtfully. You will enhance your organization's reputation—as well as your own.

11. Establish your values. Develop your own philosophy of leadership—have a clearly defined system of beliefs and practices and use them regularly, but not rigidly. Convey your philosophy consistently to your team. Expand your philosophy as you gain more experience and more

knowledge but resist fads and quick fixes in favor of long-term solutions.

12. Nurture employees and set examples. Like baseball, leadership encompasses many innings and requires a strong team. Strong teams need to have endurance and the ability to handle—and then overcome—adversity. Columbia University President Lee Bollinger made what he knew was going to be a controversial decision when he invited Iranian President Mahmoud Ahmadinejad to speak at Columbia's New York campus. A First Amendment scholar, Bollinger was severely criticized for the invitation and for his own remarks that day, but he persevered and set an example for both faculty and students—and we learned much more about the Iranian leader as a result of Bollinger's decision to invite him to speak. Effective leaders help their teams develop these skills by teaching them informally through their own actions, and formally through leadership training programs. It's important that you share some of your successes—and failures—as part of any program.

Practically everywhere you look, the emergence of greed and the disappearance of civility and empathy are manifest. Here are a few examples of the most obvious signs:

- While politics has never been a landscape for the weak-kneed, our political parties have become increasingly polarized, debate is especially negative with vicious, vitriolic personal attacks and name-calling at their worst ever, and compromise, so vital to progress, has become a dirty word.

- Social media encourages unruly, disrespectful behavior as it allows people to hide behind a mask and be unaccountable; just read the comments section of most online articles if you are in doubt.

- Television programming, especially reality TV, is dummying down viewers as frequent displays of rudeness and poor manners have become the norm; as we all know, it is all about ratings, not what is good for society.

- News media, once the vanguards of fairness and balance, have substituted hard-hitting, in-depth, and factual reporting with "entertainment" fluff.

No leader wants to fail but not enough yet realize the indisputable linkage between treating everyone with genuine respect and recognition of their worth and the organization's sustained competitive advantage—the difference between positive and inclusive versus negative and alienating. How we speak with one another and work together are essential for fostering greater collaboration and innovation.

An organization that assumes its workplace is viewed by stakeholders and shareholders as vanguards of mutual respect, dignity, self-control, and cooperation and where bullying, backstabbing, and verbal or physical abuse don't exist should take a closer look—they may be surprised by what they see. It is human nature to want to see a connection between our work, our contributions day in and day out, and the organization's successful attainment of its goals. In other words, we want to feel appreciated. During the COVID-19 outbreak in 2020, organizations that truly cared about their employees provided paid sick leave and allowed employees to work from home—they put people above profits. The pandemic made it clear that benefits like paid sick leave are not just good for employee morale, they're good for the bottom line: employees don't get other employees sick, and consumers are more apt to support organizations that take care of their employees. Organizations that are dedicated to developing positive and inclusive workplaces succeed more often than those that don't.

*"Integrity is telling myself the truth. And honesty
is telling the truth to other people."*

—SPENCER JOHNSON

CHAPTER 7

HONOR THE TRUTH

The truth is one of the cornerstones of leadership. Even a white lie can undermine your structure, and cause it to collapse.

During World War II, correspondents like Ernie Pyle covered the European and Pacific wars from the front lines. Howard K. Smith and others reported directly on the Battle of the Bulge, the surrender of Berlin, and the liberation of the Nazi death camps, which bore witness to the horror of the Holocaust. As members of the media, their goal was to deliver the truth.

The media examines, evaluates, reports, even questions the events and policies that govern actions, whether in the battlefield at home or abroad. They represent truth in action. Sadly, in more recent times, reporters have been kept at a distance and news coverage has often been after-the-fact, and at times misleading or even inaccurate. In some instances, they have been entirely cut out.

The constitutional guarantees of a free press and open exchange of ideas stand in stark contrast to the policies of those who use terror, secrecy, and falsehoods to threaten the world's democracies. Now, more than ever, the media must be free to cover events accurately and responsibly without restrictions that make little sense.

We live in a twenty-four-hour news cycle, one that provides instant access to events around the globe. These changes necessitate a heightened responsibility on the part of the media, especially when details must remain classified and individuals need to be protected both physically and emotionally. But the need for caution does not negate the right of the media to provide factual accounts of events, or an excuse for leaders to not tell the truth.

"The first casualty when war comes is truth," said California U.S. Senator Hiram Johnson in 1917.

"We have to uphold a free press and freedom of speech," as former President Barack Obama stated, "because, in the end, lies and misinformation are no match for the truth."

When organizations suppress the truth—whether that organization is the military, a corporation, or even a media outlet—all stakeholders suffer: employees, customers, and shareholders. Whether in business, government, or the media, true leaders seek the truth to communicate an accurate accounting to others—in other words, to relate the truth with a high degree of certainty.

We are living in a time unlike any other when the sheer number and viciousness of conspiracy theorists and "fake news" true believers know no bounds; where so-called "leaders" regularly espouse hatred of many traditional media and treat reporters with disgust and disrespect. Wild, unsubstantiated claims bombard the news waves every day and night. And, all too often, they are going unchecked, with more accepting the ratcheted-up rhetoric of lying and deceit.

Like all of us, traditional or mainstream media are imperfect and make mistakes. And when they do, they must acknowledge their errors. Unfortunately, with the advent of the internet and the increasing influence of social media, the line between actual news and opinion has become increasingly blurred. Years ago, newspaper editors would expect reporters to obtain two or three reliable sources to corroborate an important story they were going to file. Reporters followed rules or at least guidelines. Along with their editors, they were trained to understand that the reader's trust in their publication depended on the integrity and honesty of those providing the news. Regrettably, I can't remember the last time a reporter owned up to a mistake he or she made. Accountability must apply to both the news media and to our leaders at every level.

To paraphrase what my colleague Norm Hartman once said, reporters and editors must increasingly hold our leaders accountable for real answers rather than change-the-subject techniques that are taught in basic media training.

When you are the press secretary to the President of the United States, or the public affairs officer for a Fortune 100 company, much of your success relies upon your ability to effectively communicate with the media. As a former public affairs officer in the naval reserve and the private sector, I understand the very real challenges of being a conduit between the media and the organization you represent. However, if there's one lesson I've learned, it is that credibility, respect, and integrity are paramount. Without these qualities, reporters will always second-guess you, and you will have difficulty getting your message heard.

One of the tenets of the founders of the U.S. was to ensure that no one, including the President, would ever be able to secure absolute power. Freedom of the press plays a major part in guaranteeing that the U.S. remains a democracy. Working with the media is seldom easy, whether you agree or disagree with what they are reporting.

Like many of you, I suspect, I was taught to not only place a very high value on the importance of a free press, but to depend on it. Inherent in that trust, however, was to make sound judgments about what I read, listened to, or watched, always carefully evaluating its veracity as best as I could determine.

Changes in media organizations—new and old—have been frequent and profound. And, the process continues. With the decline of dailies across our country, a few mainline news organizations like *The Wall Street Journal*, *The Washington Post*, and *The New York Times* seem to be holding their own, in print and online. They appear to be as committed as ever to the pursuit of the truth. That said, they are being challenged as never before.

When Mike McCurry was press secretary to President Bill Clinton, he used his dry sense of humor, combined with an interpersonal style and a high degree of cooperation, to enable him to succeed in his position. He told me that his goal was always to provide the media with honest, credible information, and that he worked arduously inside the White House to get key players, including the president, to level with him. Mr. McCurry never felt as if he had been blindsided. He was not afraid of the truth.

Take a lesson from McCurry. If you want to get your message out, it is important to work *with* the outlets you use for communicating your message. You cannot expect the media to listen to you if you are not perceived as credible, respectful, and truthful. What my fellow public affairs colleagues and I have learned is that if you embrace the following, you will likely enjoy a more productive relationship with your constituents, whether they are the media, employees, customers, or shareholders:

- *Be consistent.* Just because you do something every day doesn't mean you're being consistent. If media briefings or employee communications are perceived as unreliable or in constant chaos, your message will never be heard. According to Bill Wilson, a former naval reserve public affairs captain and television newsman with many decades of experience, if you want your message to be heard, it needs consistency. Get your facts—and story—straight. Always tell the truth.

- *Be empathetic.* If you've been in someone else's shoes, you'll have a better understanding of the challenges that person or persons face. As a former newsman and company CEO, Wilson understood how the media worked, and as a result, could empathize with them—even if they didn't always see eye-to-eye. If you are a corporate CEO, you may not have experienced what your line workers or customers have, but you can show respect for their experiences and try to put yourself in their shoes. Interestingly, Wilson learned the importance of trust early on as a pilot and now as a flight instructor.

- *Respect your audience.* The media is on the front line, as are your employees. It's not your job to do a reporter's or employee's job for him or her. But it is important to be responsive—and honest. If not, your reputation will suffer. Respect the needs of your constituents, and they will generally respond in kind.

- *Be honest.* According to Larry Ames, former assistant sports editor at *The Boston Globe*, retired sports editor of the *Ventura County Star*, and author of the book *Never Dull*, it is crucial to be open in all matters: "Honesty, quickly delivered, is all you ever need to know." When your constituents know you're being upfront, even if it's to say that you can't comment on something or share information, your honesty leads to trust. Trust is essential in any relationship.

- *Learn from your mistakes.* Everyone makes mistakes—it's what makes us human. Learning from them makes us better at what we do. If you make a mistake, own up to it, correct it, and move on. And be sure you do it quickly! Don't ever let a mistake linger because you are embarrassed or hope it will just disappear. And certainly don't ever lie about it—not even a white lie! People will respect you for it, and understand. After all, it is no secret that they also make mistakes. The difference is that the real professionals are not afraid to admit it, make it right, and move on. Continuous learning is important to working with reporters.

David Muir, anchor of *ABC World News Tonight*, is known for his credibility, honesty, and unbiased and apolitical journalism. Muir said, "Peter Jennings was the James Bond of evening news, and I always wanted to be that. His evening news was really a conversation with America, and I hope that's something I can achieve."

True leaders understand the value of communicating honestly with clients, constituents, and even those who disagree with them. According to Norm Hartman, a business pioneer in media training and crisis communication, as well as an award-winning broadcast journalist, there is an obligation that arises out of the presidency to answer questions unless personnel matters, or matters involving national security, prevent you from doing so. James Madison, the fourth president of the United States, once wrote that freedom of the press is the right that guarantees all the others. And, as we try to forge ahead along a path fraught with peril from practically every direction, the stakes for the U.S.—and for the entire global community—have never been higher.

A particularly effective leader is Jacinda Ardern of New Zealand. Few heads of state have responded as skillfully and sensitively as the 39-year-old prime minister did after the horrific attack on two Christchurch mosques that killed fifty Muslims on March 15, 2019. She then pushed and gained approval of sweeping gun legislation to strengthen the safety of all her countrymen and women. In 2020, her competency, empathy, and dispatch were largely responsible for the low rate of infection of COVID-19 in her country.

"When they go low, we go high."

—MICHELLE OBAMA

CHAPTER 8

THE GOLDEN RULE
STILL MATTERS

Today's Congress is so starkly divided along partisan lines, it's hard to imagine a time when legislators worked together on a regular basis—co-sponsoring bills and compromising with the other party to pass important legislation. In 2020, it took a global pandemic (COVID-19) to enact into law a series of public health and economic measures to do so. Now may be a good time to remember those public servants whose bipartisanship and courage made us a better nation.

On June 1, 1950, as McCarthyism began to divide Congress and America, Sen. Margaret Chase Smith, a Republican from Maine, issued her "Declaration of Conscience," asking for bipartisan cooperation to protect national security. "It is high time that we stopped thinking politically as Republicans and Democrats about elections," she said, "and started thinking patriotically as Americans about national security based on individual freedom."

The joint efforts of Sen. Richard G. Lugar, a Republican from Indiana, and Sen. Sam Nunn, a Georgia Democrat, helped bring about the deactivation of thousands of nuclear and chemical weapons left over from the Cold War. After he left Congress, Lugar established the Lugar Center, a think tank dedicated to good governance and bipartisanship. Nunn still serves as co-chair of the Nuclear Threat Initiative, a nonpartisan organization he co-founded in 2001 that fights the use and spread of weapons of mass destruction.

President Gerald Ford was a moderate Republican who was known for bipartisan leadership throughout his twenty-five years in the House. Ford stoked controversy when he pardoned Richard Nixon but did what he thought was best for what he thought was best to heal the nation after the years of the Watergate saga; his own political career suffered as a result. Ford later received the Presidential Medal of Freedom and the John F. Kennedy Profiles in Courage Award.

Sen. Philip Hart, a Michigan Democrat known—by both parties—as the "Conscience of the Senate," was a World War II combat veteran who championed the 1964 Civil Rights Act and 1965 Voting Rights Act. Hart was respected for standing up for what he believed was right, rather than what was politically expedient.

Sen. Olympia Snowe, a Republican from Maine, was a pragmatic and independent senator who often broke ranks with her party. She served as co-chair of the Senate Centrist Coalition, a bipartisan group. "We can have our differences here, but we ought to be able to talk with each other without being punished for it," Snowe said in 2001.

New York Rep. Shirley Chisholm, a Democrat, was known to criticize Democratic and Republican congressional leaders alike. Chisholm also defended to fellow African Americans the need to work with white politicians to get things done: "We still have to engage in compromise, the highest of all arts."

Finally, Republican Sen. John McCain from Arizona criticized his party and president on several issues, spoke out for civility, and also maintained close friendships with Democrats such as Sen. Edward M. (Ted) Kennedy. Today, McCain's family carries on his spirit of bipartisanship through a social media and action campaign called #ActsOfCivility. McCain's widow, Cindy McCain, urges on the website johnmccain.com: "Commit to something larger than yourself. Reach across the aisle. Break the barrier. Come together for civil engagement." Wise words indeed. And sorely needed ones.

Contrast these examples with what is more commonly seen today. The level of rudeness in this country has reached a fever pitch. Why? Because, it's become too easy for rudeness to morph into outright hate.

Political parties have become increasingly polarized. Disparity in compensation between corporate executives and those on the shop floor has never been wider. Social media encourages people to be unaccountable for their behavior by allowing them to post vitriol online behind the safe mask of anonymity. Television programming, especially "reality" TV, frequently encourages rudeness and disrespect. Even the news media, once the vanguard of fairness and objectivity, too often has become nothing more than entertainment fluff or the biased thoughts of "opinion hosts" posing as journalists. Tolerance for different perspectives has evaporated and too many disputes end violently and tragically.

In my book, *Truth, Trust + Tenacity: How Ordinary People Become Extraordinary Leaders*, I talk about civil discourse and how it's often portrayed as a weakness when, in fact, it takes much more resolve to compromise and show respect than it does to be rude and unbending. Unfortunately, too many people equate being rude as a sign of being superior. Nothing could be further from the truth.

The results of rudeness are real: in the workplace, employees who are subjected to this type of disrespectful behavior put in less effort and work fewer hours. They often take out their frustrations on other employees, as well as clients or customers, family members, even strangers. There is a reason the phrase "misery loves company" is so popular—this type of behavior is contagious. Productivity, and ultimately profits, suffer.

Consider the following examples of rude behavior we all see far too often today:

- Parents who assume store employees or restaurant servers are there to babysit or clean up after their children. Mom and Dad ignore their kids' behavior and get offended when they are called out on it. Children who observe this behavior assume it's acceptable to be rude and that the rules of etiquette don't apply to them.

- People who keep you waiting for no real reason. Two of my former bosses regularly kept people waiting simply because they could. They wanted to ensure that everyone knew who was in charge.

- Aggressive drivers who weave in and out of traffic, cut you off, or text while driving—and then swear at you if you point it out. These drivers are creating dangerous and often life-threatening situations.

- People who don't know how to say "thank you." How many times have you held the door for someone without any acknowledgment? Not only is this rude, it's also a sign of stupidity and arrogance. For some reason, certain people feel it's beneath them to hold the door open for another, or to even recognize that there's someone there, letting the door hit the next person as it closes.

- People who litter, throw trash from their car window, leave the office break room a mess, and drop a used cigarette wherever they walk.

While these examples may seem inconsequential in a world with far bigger problems, they are ones we can all relate to. Just as with hate, no one is born rude—it is a learned behavior that can be just as destructive if left unchecked.

Just as there are people who demonstrate rude behavior on a daily basis, there are others who remind us that humility and deference for others can go a long way towards being a "good neighbor."

Arnold Palmer was known for his constantly attacking golf swing, easy smile, matchless charisma, unstinting generosity, and business acumen. He had an uncanny ability to relate to all people, regardless of their position. Palmer understood the power of respect and civility: he cherished and appreciated his fans and treated them well, selflessly giving his time to sign autographs for hours when asked. No wonder his followers were known as Arnie's Army.

Arnold Palmer never forgot his modest Pennsylvania roots or the discipline he learned throughout his enlistment in the United States Coast Guard. Men and women alike admired him. I closely followed Palmer's career, first in the gallery when fresh out of the Navy and later as a PGA Tour marshal. When I met him, like countless others, I felt like I was the most important person in his world.

His genuine humility and strength of character are relevant today, especially in the business community. Too many so-called business "leaders" don't lead. They boss. They demean. They disparage. They don't motivate, and they lack personal integrity. True leaders inspire. They encourage risks without repercussions, and they treat everyone with dignity and respect—just as Arnold Palmer did with his fans and later with all his business associates.

Palmer may not go down in history as the planet's best golfer, and I bet Palmer would be OK with that. In fact, he would no doubt tell you it's more important to be remembered as one of the world's best citizens. As he once said, "Success in this game depends less on strength of body than strength of mind and character." I always liked the cut of his jib!

Anthony Fauci, M.D., Director of Allergy and Infectious Diseases at NIH during the 2020 COVID-19 pandemic, was quoted as saying, "Some people feel, you make the case. If they listen to you, fine. If they don't, that's it. That's not what leadership is. Leadership is trying to continue to make a case." During a time of heightened fear and uncertainty, he proved to be a true leader: honest in his communications and forthright in his assessments. Like Arnold Palmer, Dr. Fauci demonstrated strength of character.

It's not difficult to be a good neighbor, elected official, parent, employer, or employee—and it's certainly more satisfying than being rude. The good news is learned behaviors, including rudeness, can be changed:

- Recognize that sometimes the rude person is *you*. Think before you act. Apologize if you act before you think.

- Don't overreact when others are rude towards you. Let it go, walk away, don't take it personally. If you feel you must, politely call it to their attention (and then drop it).

- Finally, think more about your own actions in your daily life, especially on the job. It's hard work to be more conscious of your actions instead of simply going through the motions. Being civil requires one to be more aware, take responsibility, and consider the repercussions.

Eric Hoffer, recipient of the Presidential Medal of Freedom, and author of ten books including *The True Believer* (1951), may have said it best: "Rudeness is the weak man's imitation of strength." The next time a colleague or stranger opens the door, thank them. Better yet, make it a point to open the door for them.

"Two things define you. Your patience when you have nothing, and your attitude when you have everything."

—GEORGE BERNARD SHAW

CHAPTER 9

UNLOCK THE POWER OF PATIENCE

Throughout this book, as well as in my previous four books, I discuss the characteristics of leadership, some of which include strong communication skills, integrity, attention to detail, the ability to compromise, civility, and respect. There's another characteristic that doesn't immediately come to mind but should: *patience*.

Patience is often thought of as a weakness when it comes to leadership. Leaders are expected to make split-second decisions, and move on to the next solution if the current one isn't working. Obsession with quarterly returns and instant gratification prohibit us from taking more heed than risk when making decisions.

If you look at the characteristics of some of the world's greatest leaders, you may notice what I did: purpose, approachability, tolerance, independence, empathy, nurturing nature, confidence, and endurance. It's not a coincidence that these words make up the acronym *patience*. It's also not a coincidence that these traits are found more in female leaders than male leaders. In fact, one study by Zenger Folkman reported in *Harvard Business Review* concluded that women outscored men on seventeen of the nineteen capabilities that differentiate excellent leaders from average or poor ones. Part of the reason is that they had to work harder for longer periods of time—in other words, they were patient out of necessity!

Purpose. Patient leaders understand that having a purpose—and sticking to it—is essential if you want meaningful change. No one illustrates this more than Germany's Chancellor Angela Merkel. While her tenure hasn't been perfect and she has faced many challenges, during her time in office Merkel led her country from intolerance to tolerance; never wavered from her purpose of ensuring that Germany remains a key player on the world stage, often leading from behind or with very little support. Merkel has been steadfast, straightforward, and not afraid to tell-it-like it is—all qualities of being purposeful. She understood the essence of purpose: "Purpose—not the leader, authority, or power—is what creates and animates a community. It is what makes people willing to do the hard tasks of innovation together and work through the inevitable conflict and tension."

Approachability. Patient leaders are open-minded and open to change; they understand the value in being accessible. Indra Nooyi, former Chairperson and CEO of PepsiCo, was known for writing personal notes to employees' parents—she understood the strength of reaching out to people at a more human and personal level. Approachable leaders take a more human-centric approach to leading—they understand that effective leaders don't exploit, they encourage. Nooyi understood that being a demagogue wouldn't work, and would, in fact, alienate customers, clients, and employees. Under her leadership, PepsiCo was open to listening to what their customers wanted and began offering more healthful products in addition to their tried and true staples.

Tolerance. Patient leaders know that being open-minded often leads to positive long-term solutions. Tolerant leaders understand the benefits of being broad-minded in accomplishing goals; they know that intolerance stunts growth, while tolerance powers it. Getting along isn't always easy. While most people probably haven't heard of Hamtramck, Michigan, it has the distinction of having the country's first majority-Muslim city council. Like its neighbor, Detroit, Hamtramck has had its share of problems, not the least of which is dealing with the fear that comes with change. Hamtramck's mayor, Karen Majewski, recognizes these challenges but knows that by being tolerant and welcoming others, you can affect change in a way that will help everyone. Majewski acknowledges that learning to be tolerant of others isn't always easy, and is often uncomfortable, but in the end we all benefit by taking advantage of individual strengths instead of focusing on individual differences.

Independence. Patient leaders are independent—they are honest and straightforward, and in some cases even defiant. Rosa Parks became a symbol of civil rights when she refused to give up her seat to a white bus passenger. Parks was quoted as saying, "I was tired of giving in." Her single act of independence changed history and thrust her into a leadership role she wasn't expecting (despite her previous activism within the NAACP). Parks' defiance fueled a movement that eventually led to passage of the Civil Rights Act of 1964 and made her a voice heard around the world. Leadership evolves from all walks of life and from within each of us—it's not reserved for CEOs or four-star generals. Parks continued her fight for equal rights until her death at the age of ninety-two.

Empathy. Patient leaders are compassionate and concerned about others. Like approachability, being empathetic isn't a sign of weakness—it's a sign of maturity and confidence. No one exemplifies this characteristic better than Mother Teresa. Like Rosa Parks, Mother Teresa was not the stereotypical leader that often comes to mind. She didn't have an MBA, never served political office, and didn't have any armed services experience. In fact, many of the most effective leaders in this world do not. Mother Teresa felt a calling to help "the poorest of the poor," a mission that continues to this day long after her death. Starting in 1946 when she first felt her calling, Mother Teresa expanded her reach to include thousands of sisters who helped thousands of destitute citizens of Calcutta. Her efforts included hospices for the dying as well as those suffering from leprosy—populations which had often been ignored before Mother Teresa's actions.

Nurturing nature. Patient leaders know that by encouraging and supporting others, the change that follows can have a significant and positive impact. Sheryl Sandberg, COO of Facebook, is an example of someone who knows how to lead and nurture. While clearly ambitious, Sandberg doesn't railroad over people, instead choosing to be a true team player. She is a compassionate advocate of women's rights—and remains undaunted even as she's criticized for being part of the "one percent." Instead of exhibiting the bad behavior that certain presidential candidates and politicians exhibit, Sandberg shows us that by remaining levelheaded and encouraging, you can achieve your goals—and more. She uses her stature and position to help—not hinder—others. Under Sandberg's tenure, Facebook moved from unprofitable to profitable. Even after the untimely death of her husband, she remains undaunted in her pursuit of equality in the workplace for women.

Confidence. Patient leaders are cool and self-assured—without being cocky and conceited. Malala Yousafzai, a 2014 recipient of the Nobel Peace Prize, exemplified this when she was shot, point-blank, by a would-be assassin. Not only did she not succumb to her injuries, she did not succumb to continued threats—instead, the experience buoyed her. Yousafzai has been unstoppable in her quest to secure educational freedom and equal rights for women around the world. With her father, Ziauddin Yousafzai, the Malala Fund promotes the right for all women to receive an education and be treated equally. Instead of giving up, and giving in, her experience gave her the confidence needed to change the world. Malala knows that fundamental change does not happen overnight—but it does happen as long as you have confidence.

Endurance. Patient leaders don't give up; they understand that real and lasting change goes beyond short-term gains. Patient leaders know what it means to endure and be persistent: the University of Tennessee's former women's basketball coach, Pat Summitt, understood that surviving and thriving would take time and tenacity. While patience isn't usually a quality associated with Summitt, in fact she exhibited a key trait—endurance. Early in her career Summitt washed her teams' clothes and drove the van that took them to their games. At a time when women's basketball was in its infancy, she persevered because she wanted her team to succeed. She knew it would take time, but she never wavered from her fortitude. She knew breaking down the barriers of the old boys' club of college basketball would take endurance. Summitt had 1,098 career wins, the most in college basketball history when she retired.

Of course, leaders of both sexes have, and do, exhibit these traits, and not all female leaders are patient. But we can learn an important lesson by studying these leaders, and how they used their fortitude to meet their goals using patience instead of impetuousness.

GRATITUDE

"A genuine leader is not a searcher for consensus but a molder of consensus."

—MARTIN LUTHER KING JR.

CHAPTER 10

DON'T BE A JERK

Just because you're the boss doesn't mean you know how to lead. A few hours of instant leadership training doesn't qualify you. Your "natural knack" doesn't qualify you. The fact that you simply fell into the job doesn't qualify you.

Throughout my career in a variety of sectors reporting to all types of decision-makers, I have seen many kinds of people—good and bad—in action. I also have dealt with a few bosses who were philanderers, racists, bullies, and egomaniacs with anger-management problems. Many were intellectually bright, but their behaviors undermined the success their organizations could have achieved with true leadership. For example, one philanderer had an executive assistant who he insisted be promoted despite her incompetence. It turns out she had filed a sexual discrimination suit against him.

Consider how bosses versus leaders often approach workplace issues:

Issue	Leader's Approach	Boss' Approach
Organizational Success	Focuses on long-term results and positions his or her company for ongoing success.	Too concerned about the next quarter's bottom line to have a big-picture perspective.
Employee Treatment	Champions employees. Works to remove obstacles for employees, provides the necessary resources, and expedites processes to make it easier to accomplish their jobs.	Sees employees as a means to an end. Creates roadblocks that get in the way of the job, lead to pointless extra work, and create unnecessary frustration.
Communication	Connects directly with the board, shareholders, customers, suppliers, and employee base, and takes the time to listen and respond in a thoughtful and humble manner that values all these people.	Pays lip service to employees but is more focused on his or her own well-being.
Respect for Others	Shows congeniality and respect to everyone regardless of rank.	Pleasant and charming to executives, while indifferent or demeaning toward those he or she supervises. Smiles up the organization and frowns down the organization.
Conflict Resolution	Deals with conflict by channeling it to constructive ends.	Creates conflict but fails to deal with it effectively.
Behavior of Managers	Prohibits demeaning, disrespectful, or verbally abusive behavior.	Ignores demeaning, disrespectful, or verbally abusive behavior, and may exhibit it himself or herself.
Work-Life Balance	Recognizes that employees enjoy a private and personal life outside of the business and appreciates the need to maintain balance for well-being and productivity.	Overloads his or her team with many tasks and impossible due dates, then micromanages them.

Too often, leaders exhibit the behavior of adolescents instead of adults: they berate employees, sport temper tantrums, or use excessive and unnecessary foul language. In other words, they act like jerks. This type of conduct does nothing to improve employee performance, customer satisfaction, or shareholder value. In fact, it does just the opposite.

True leaders are imperturbable: They have the innate ability to remain calm in the middle of chaos. That attribute is an all-too-often ignored skill among leaders, overshadowed by today's seemingly increasing bombastic and egotistical outpourings. Imperturbable leaders know that keeping your wits during the most difficult of circumstances can diffuse previously believed irresolvable conflict, anger, and tension, and channel it into needed, constructive change.

Three people immediately come to mind as examples of imperturbable leaders, all of whom I've had the fortunate experience to have known: John A. Hannah, president of Michigan State University from 1941 to 1969, Robben W. Fleming, president of the University of Michigan from 1968 to 1978, and Carol Tomlinson-Keasey, founding chancellor of the University of California, Merced from 1999 to 2006. Although all three made an indelible mark in academia, their leadership skills are applicable to any industry.

None had big egos. They didn't need to be the center of attention or make major speeches with great rhetorical flair. They were intelligent, yet humble. At the same time, they were nobody's fool. They did many things quietly, but not in an underhanded way. They had very strong values and great fortitude rooted in their upbringing. People naturally gravitated toward them.

Their integrity and moral compasses enabled them to be transformers. Against incredible odds and opposition, Hannah built Michigan State from a campus of 6,000 students into a prestigious Big Ten university of more than 47,000. By quietly focusing on relationships, he was able to get more legislative funding for his school than other universities in the state. His leadership helped the school grow and increase its diversity. It is not coincidental that the first African American president of a predominantly white major learning institution (Dr. Clifton R. Wharton Jr.) was at Michigan State.

Under Fleming's leadership, the University of Michigan grew to become one of the country's premier and internationally respected public research universities. When Fleming took over, the Ann Arbor campus was at the forefront of campus unrest. His skill in negotiating with unmatched patience, tolerance, and reason throughout the anti-war and civil rights protests of the 1960s and early 1970s, without the violence and destruction that marred many other campuses, was nothing less than extraordinary.

Tomlinson-Keasey was given the herculean task of planning, securing funding for, and later opening a new campus, the University of California at Merced, in the middle of California's rich agricultural and culturally diverse San Joaquin Valley. With higher poverty levels, lower education levels, worsening air pollution, and a medically underserved population more problematic than in any other part of California, a new campus was needed—one that would become a powerful economic engine for the valley and the state. Tomlinson-Keasey became the university's first female to occupy the top spot at any UC branch.

Hannah knew that many Michigan State students came from families whose incomes were modest at best, so he made his apartment available to a Michigan State athlete (before athletic scholarships were the norm). He permitted different student-athletes to stay rent-free in exchange for their doing routine cleaning and cooking chores. Fleming, while chancellor at the University of Wisconsin, used his own money to bail out jailed students who were arrested for blockading a university building during a campus protest. Both men took a genuine interest in their students' welfare. How many university presidents—or CEOs for that matter—do you think would act similarly today?

Fleming spent six years in the U.S. Army in World War II but spoke out against the Vietnam War and helped spearhead international projects in Nigeria, France, Germany, and Japan. His life experiences coupled with his study of law, especially labor relations, helped forge his open, poised, and conciliatory approach to conflict. Fleming had a Lincolnesque quality. He could not be easily provoked, believing insults had to be endured because conflict usually presented opportunities for improvement.

Tomlinson-Keasey used every bit of her indefatigable spirit, high energy, stamina, and unwavering belief in youth to achieve her goals. Reluctant state legislators, working with four different gubernatorial administrations, nagging environmental issues, and a state budget crisis that delayed the opening of the campus by a year, confronted her at practically each step along the way. And so did fierce competition on the part of other UC campuses and the California State University (CSU) system vying for state appropriations and private monies, as well as often-provocative central valley pressure groups, a skeptical media, and formidable construction challenges. Tomlinson-Keasey envisioned students of immigrants, farm families, and others (often first-generation college attendees) becoming tomorrow's leaders in science, technology, medicine, engineering, and the environment as a result of the new university.

Hannah, Fleming, and Tomlinson-Keasey remained calm in the face of fierce and relentless criticism or confrontation. They committed to a larger goal than simply increasing the size of their organizations (in this case, universities)—they chose to dedicate their lives to improving the lives of both students and the surrounding community.

True leaders understand that you can accomplish a lot more by using a moral compass and demonstrating integrity than you can being a jerk.

"The best portion of a good life is the little nameless, unremembered acts of kindness and of love."

—WILLIAM WORDSWORTH

CHAPTER 11

Stop Texting, and Start Writing

More and more, when you receive a "thank you" from your boss, it's probably in the form of a text message or e-mail. And while acknowledgment of a job well done is important, regardless of whether it's electronic or handwritten, it's critical that the communication speaks to the recipient as an individual.

It's no secret that handwritten letters and notes are going the way of CDs and VCRs. This almost-lost art has been replaced by e-mail, instant messaging, Facebook status updates, tweets, and text messages—all forms of communication that are ubiquitous because we can fire them off quickly. In many cases, the tool we are using will suggest verbiage for us to use. By contrast, handwritten notes are more personal, and that personal touch is what's missing from most electronic messaging today.

According to The Radicati Group, a market research firm focused on the computer and telecommunications industry, the number of worldwide e-mail users, including both business and consumer users, will grow from over 4.0 billion in 2020 to nearly 4.5 billion by 2024. According to Statista.com, in 2018 an estimated 2.65 billion people were using social media worldwide, a number projected to increase to almost 3.1 billion in 2021. According to Business Insider, Americans send roughly 26 billion text messages *each day*.

In the business world, sending messages of recognition, congratulations, or appreciation, or directing a request or an appeal through Twitter, texting, Facebook, or e-mail, is certainly faster and easier. But what is often missing in those communications is authenticity and forethought. When you put pen to paper, you are forced to think about what you are writing because you can't simply hit the delete key.

The fact that it takes longer to write out a personal note also speaks volumes to the recipients—that you took valuable time from your busy day to write a note just for them. Not just a personal note, but a personal *handwritten* note. It's the difference between receiving a gift of a scarf, for example, from a local department store, and one that someone created especially for you. Both are thoughtful, but the handcrafted gift means more.

It is unrealistic and impractical to handwrite every note you send. However, you can take the time to make your messages more personal, and creating handwritten ones from time-to-time will remind you of the importance of what you're doing. Personal communications, including those written by hand, remain important in diplomatic circles, especially among some top government leaders. They should be as important in the business world. A truly personal note to a client, employee, supervisor, or business colleague has many benefits:

- Your note will help you stand out and be noticed and remembered in a way that the more fleeting messages can't accomplish.

- Handwritten notes especially come across as more thoughtful because you most likely had to carefully consider what to say before writing it down.

- A tweet, text, or e-mail can get quickly buried under a mountain of newer tweets, texts, and e-mails. A personal or handwritten message will be remembered for a long time, even if it gets filed away.

- Personal notes from business leaders often help strengthen employee morale, heighten productivity, facilitate interpersonal communication, and help retain team members who will feel more appreciated, leading to reduced recruiting and training costs.

Personal letters, including those written by hand, can have a powerful impact and move public opinion as well. The former CEO of Campbell's Soup, Douglas Conant, wrote more than 30,000 thank-you notes to employees over the course of his ten-year career. Frank Blake, retired CEO of Home Depot, handwrote more than 25,000 notes during his career at the home retailer. He knew he had made an impact when he himself was flooded with handwritten notes upon his retirement. Sheldon Yellen, CEO of BELFOR Holdings, Inc., a property restoration company, handwrites 9,200 cards *each year*. All these CEOs understand the impact that personalization has on employees, and ultimately on customers and shareholders—that they care. Whether they set aside several hours on a Sunday (Conant) or use downtime on flights (Yellen), these CEOs understand the importance of connecting with their employees on a more personal level.

Workplace gratitude matters. In a world filled with e-mail, 140-character tweets, and Facebook messages, low-tech can stand out in a way high-tech can't.

Former U.S. Secretary of Defense Bob Gates wrote very personal letters to survivors of fallen military personnel—letters that always conveyed a deep sense of caring to the recipient. Legendary Kansas State head football coach Bill Snyder often wrote personal letters to members of his team as well as to opposing players who got injured or performed admirably. Coach Snyder and I exchanged some personal letters before he retired.

It wasn't that the notes these leaders wrote were always written in longhand—many, if not most, were not—but that they took the time to make their communications mean something special to the individual receiving them.

After the Oakland A's baseball team and their manager, Ken Macha, parted ways, Macha received a handwritten note from managing partner Lewis Wolff wishing him well and telling him that he would "be successful at anything you do. Thanks for a great season." Macha ended up coming to an agreement with the A's and stayed with the team. While there were other factors involved in him staying, Wolff's note had a profound impact. Adding a personal touch to whatever you do can have unexpected—and sometimes amazing—results.

One sometimes overlooked way of conveying a different kind of personal message is the chairman or CEO's letter to shareholders in the organization's annual report. For many years, the responsibility for producing the annual report including the letter was mine. Historically, many annual reports have been either boring, extravagant, or a combination of both. Many top leaders delegated the production of the report and letter to either staff or an outside PR firm. On the other hand, some letters were especially noteworthy for their originality, including those from Warren Buffett. The Berkshire Hathaway leader's letters are known for their instructive, insightful, and interesting prose. Jeff Bezos of Amazon, Howard Schultz of Starbucks, and Jamie Dimon of JP Morgan have penned some rather transparent, thoughtful, and transformative ones. So, too, have Brian Cornell of Target and Richard Branson of Virgin.

For as long as I can remember, I have believed in the practice of saying "thank you" to others as a sincere gesture of appreciation. My parents instilled in my brother and me the importance of writing and sending notes to those who gave us gifts of one kind or another. Later, when I wrote letters on my computer, I often penned a handwritten note near the bottom of the letter when printed to reinforce my intent.

For many years to this day I have used a colorful card with two signal flags and the words *Bravo Zulu* below the flags to commend members of my team, as well as others, for especially noteworthy achievements or humanitarian acts. "Bravo Zulu" in Navy jargon means "Well Done!" On the backside of the card, I pen a handwritten note. These notes are personal, often unexpected, and based on the feedback I've received, appreciated.

Purposely, they are used when the situation fully warrants it; that is, so it is truly meaningful—I am careful not to dilute the desired impact by overuse. Some of the examples for using these attractive cards are:

- Service above and beyond
- Achievement (major work milestone, academic, athletic, political, volunteer, community)
- Overcoming adversity
- Special acts of kindness
- Courageous behavior
- Heartfelt condolences
- Major celebratory occasions

Some of the busiest people I know who have or have had very demanding jobs write personal notes: General Joseph F. Dunford Jr., USMC (ret.), Chairman of the Joint Chiefs of Staff; David A. Brandon, Chairman, Domino's Pizza and later Chairman and CEO, Toys "R" Us; Ora H. Pescovitz, M.D., President, Oakland University and former CEO, University of Michigan Health System; Dick Gould, John L. Hinds Director of Tennis (ret)., Stanford University and coach of seventeen Stanford Men's NCAA Championship Teams; Howdy Holmes, president and CEO, Chelsea Milling Co. ("JIFFY" Mix); and the late Rich

DeVos, cofounder, Amway Corporation and owner, Orlando Magic (NBA). I have kept some of the most moving notes I've received during the past forty years and often wished I'd kept more of them.

The business world could gain a lot by recapturing this lost art. The next time you want to congratulate someone for a job well done, thank your boss for giving you a raise, inspire a newly hired worker, show appreciation to a client, or show concern for someone having a particularly difficult time, make it personal and better yet—write it by hand. You will be pleasantly surprised by the effect it has.

*"Architecture and any art can transform
a person, even save someone."*

—FRANK GEHRY

CHAPTER 12

EMBRACE THE TRANSFORMATIVE POWER OF THE ARTS

Frank Gehry, arguably the world's most famous living architect, is well-known for his bold designs including the Guggenheim Museum (Bilbao) in Spain and the Dancing House in Prague. Gehry's influence can also be felt where I live (Southern California): the Binoculars Building (originally the Chiat/Day building), Spiller House, Cabrillo Marine Aquarium, California Aerospace Museum, and the Walt Disney Concert Hall.

Paul Revere Williams (1894-1980), another Southern California architect, is best known for his graceful designs that transformed the Beverly Wilshire Apartment Hotel into the iconic Beverly Wilshire Hotel. He went on to design the original St. Jude's Children's Research Hospital building, the Second Baptist Church, the 28th Street YMCA, and numerous private homes.

While both of these Los Angeles-based architects came of age during the twentieth century and both attended USC—albeit in different decades—they had distinctly different styles. Gehry's buildings are sexy, colorful, and fun. Williams' designs are elegant, stylized, and practical. Both attract attention because their buildings stand out as visual masterpieces.

Paul R. Williams, the first African-American architect to practice west of the Mississippi, designed more than 3,000 buildings in Southern California and elsewhere. The recipient of many awards, he had to conquer numerous racial challenges. During his early career, many whites were uncomfortable sitting next to a black man so Williams learned to draft upside down so he could sit across the desk from his client, who would see his work right-side up. In 1923, Williams became the first African-American member of the American Institute of Architects (AIA). In WWII, he was an architect for the Department of the Navy. In 2017, this highly skilled draftsman and artistic genius posthumously received AIA's Gold Medal, their highest award, and the first awarded to an African-American.

While their design aesthetics were at opposite ends of the spectrum, both Gehry and Williams seamlessly integrate form and function. Both men understood the importance of art in creating workplaces and homes—they knew that the right package inspires. Good design triggers emotions. It can make you feel happy, empowered, inspired, or comfortable.

Artists are adept at creativity, innovation, planning, time management, discipline, cooperation, problem solving, and inspiring others. They thrive on collaborating with a culturally diverse group of colleagues and are not afraid to challenge the status quo, as both Gehry and Williams have done. Artists must adapt to fluid situations because their livelihoods often depend on it. Not surprisingly, these are all skills businesses can benefit from.

In his book *Steve Jobs*, author Walter Isaacson described how the Apple co-founder audited classes in calligraphy and music, as well as physics and electronics, after dropping out of college. These classes had a tremendous influence on how he approached the design of his products. Many of Apple's most talented engineers were accomplished in music or some other art form.

The importance of art in the training of medical students has also been well documented. Universities including Harvard and Yale require their medical students to tour art galleries as part of art appreciation classes. The goal is to help those students hone their observation skills and become more flexible thinkers who can make better diagnoses. A review of Harvard students who took the course found that students made 40 percent more clinical observations, which could potentially lead to more efficient and less expensive care.

According to the results of a 2019 study by Dr. Natasha Kirkham, a senior lecturer in psychology and researcher at the Centre for Brain and Cognitive Development at Birkbeck, University of London, even kids as young as three years old can have experienced the benefits of live theatre performance by improved levels of understanding and academic performance, and positive social change—all of which bode well as those kids become working adults.

The melding of arts with other disciplines is common in programs such as the Stamps School of Art & Design at the University of Michigan. The art and design faculty conduct a wide range of research projects working with scientists, doctors, information architects, climatologists, and others to solve real-world issues.

According to The pARTnership Movement, partnering with the arts helps businesses in a broad range of ways, often where traditional business schools cannot:

- It fosters creativity, a top skill sought by employers— companies that give to the arts recognize that the arts stimulate creative thinking, problem solving, and team building.

- It leads to stronger, more vibrant communities that attract and engage employees—according to the National Endowment for the Arts, the arts contribute more than $760 billion to the U.S. economy. Communities that want to attract top employees and grow their local economies invest heavily in local arts and culture. According to a 2018 Conference Board report, "Business Contributions to the Arts," 35 percent of companies surveyed reported that supporting the arts helped them retain employees.

- It helps businesses build market share, enhance their brand, and reach new customers. The arts can be used to build a powerful presence and engage with multiple stakeholders in a way traditional marketing and advertising efforts cannot. According to the same Conference Board study referenced above, 79 percent of businesses say involvement with the arts improves the quality of life in the communities in which they operate, and 39 percent reported that it advanced their organizational objectives.

Apart from supporting the arts and hiring employees from arts organizations, *integrating* the arts into your workplace can improve workplace performance and relationships by inspiring spontaneity, creativity, and ingenuity.

Building relationships in the workplace doesn't require climbing walls, paint ball, or falling backwards into waiting hands. Sometimes, we simply need a mental break from the routine to get our minds cleared of the suffocating strategic, financial, and operational demands that are part and parcel of organizational life.

Art has a positive—and powerful—physiological impact on the brain. Research has shown that fine and performing arts can help reduce blood pressure while improving one's focus and outlook on their job or about life in general. Art can help us look at something with a different perspective by stimulating creativity and thoughtful observation. Art can combat tunnel vision, and help make a cold, sterile work environment feel more inspiring. Art can stimulate us to think more creatively (i.e., "outside the box").

One of the people who really opened my eyes to the power of the arts in business was Frank Merlotti Sr., president and CEO of Steelcase, the global leader in office furniture. I was a Senior VP at Butterworth Hospital in Grand Rapids, Michigan, and Merlotti was on the hospital's board of trustees. He chaired the board's Cost Containment Committee that I was responsible for staffing. Our relationship gave me the opportunity to visit the Steelcase offices many times.

Steelcase has long understood the interrelationships among art forms, design, functionality, creativity, and workplace efficiency. If you ever want to see one of the most effective blends of art, architecture, and business success, visit the Steelcase corporate headquarters in Grand Rapids. The entire business environment delights the senses and heightens the desire for discovery. This is no big shock, considering that Robert Pew, the former board chairman of Steelcase, and his partner, Frank Merlotti Sr., the former president and CEO, were leaders who believed in (and practiced) humility, excellence, kindness, and being team players while delivering quality and value to customers.

The benefits of the arts are often unrecognized and viewed as a frivolous use of funds. However, the ability to think clearly and creatively is anything but frivolous—the good news is that you don't need to spend much money to reap the benefits. Here are a few simple suggestions for integrating the arts into your workplace:

1. *Include music in your place of business.* The Nordstrom department stores were well-known for their pianist-in-residence. The pianist was there for the benefit of customers, but associates benefited just as much. Install

a music system for the lunchroom or a conference room and ask your team what type of music they prefer, and incorporate their ideas. Choose a selection that will appeal to all so that people can enjoy some music during their workday or lunch hour. The result will be a more relaxed and refreshed team—one that will be more effective at problem solving.

2. *Plant a small garden outdoors or on a patio.* If you have the funds, consult a landscape expert to create a soothing Zen garden—or better yet, ask employees for their own ideas. Be sure to include tables, chairs, and benches so people can enjoy their lunch there. Don't have any outdoor space? Transform a break room with beautiful plants, potted trees, and flowers. Place greenery throughout the workplace. The result will be a calmer team, better able to focus. And don't be surprised if they start meeting regularly in the newly installed greenspace.

3. *Create an art gallery at your workplace.* Consult a local gallery owner or artist to help bring in paintings, sculptures, professional photography, or other pieces of art for display the way many hospitals do. If you don't have the budget to purchase pieces, invite local artists, art students, or even employees to display their works

on a rotating basis in the hallways at your place of work. Chances are the artists will be thrilled: you get a rotating gallery and they get free exposure—it's a win-win for all. The result will be a less-sterile environment that will inspire your team and may even elicit conversations among team members viewing the art—conversations that wouldn't have otherwise taken place.

Overall, the arts are a huge—but often unappreciated—driver of the economy in every state and city, in terms of consumer spending on activities like concerts and symphony performances, theater shows, museum exhibits, local film festivals and the many artistic events people from all walks of life enjoy year-round. PBS reported that a government analysis shows that the arts account for almost $900 billion of our gross domestic product (GDP) and over five million jobs nationwide. The 2020 COVID-19 pandemic laid bare just how many millions of dollars are spent yearly on the arts and how many Americans are employed in arts-related jobs, when theaters closed, concerts and festivals were canceled, and museums were shuttered. Support for the arts is essential for our GDP.

Incorporating the arts into your business, and business planning, is certainly worth the return you'll see on your investment—whether it's supporting local arts organizations, hiring employees with arts backgrounds, or integrating the arts into your workplace. The bottom-line impact is inescapable—if you want to attract customers or retain employees, your business needs the arts.

REFERENCES

FRONT MATTER

Ambrose, Stephen E. *Eisenhower: Soldier and President* (New York: Simon & Schuster), October 15, 1991.

CHAPTER 1

CAF Red Tail Squadron. "Mrs. Roosevelt goes for a Ride." Red Wing, MN.

Collamer, Nancy. "The 5 Hidden Career Lessons in 'HiddenFigures.'" *Next Avenue*. Forbes.com, February 6, 2017.

Graham, Shawn. "3 Lessons Every Manager Can Learn from 'Moneyball.'" *Fast Co.*, September 28, 2011.

Stahl, Leslie. "What the Last Nuremberg Prosecutor Alive Wants the World to Know." *60 Minutes,* June 30, 2019.

CHAPTER 2

https://girlpowermarketing.com/womens-purchasing-power/

CHAPTER 3

Weick, Karl E. and Kathleen M. Sutcliffe. *Managing the Unexpected* (San Francisco: Jossey-Bass), 2001.

CHAPTER 4

Berman, Larry. *Zumwalt: The Life and Times of Admiral Elmo Russell "Bud" Zumwalt, Jr.* (New York: HarperCollins), October 2012.

Eich, Ritch K. and William E. Wiethoff. "Toward a Model of Hierarchical Change." *Communication Quarterly 27*, no.1 (1979): 29-37.

https://www.findagrave.com/cgi-bin/
fg.cgi?page=gr&Grid=2067

Senor, Dan and Saul Singer. *Start-Up Nation: The Story of Israel's Economic Miracle.* (New York: Hachette Book Group), 2009.

CHAPTER 5

https://www.pewsocialtrends.org/2019/03/21/public-sees-an-america-in-decline-on-many-fronts/

Tichy, Noel and Eli Cohen. *The Leadership Engine.* (New York: HarperCollins), 1997.

CHAPTER 7

Eich, Ritch K. "Once again, truth is the first casualty." *San Jose Mercury News,* May 7, 2002.

Personal Interviews conducted from 2011 to the present with Norm Hartman, Mike McCurry, Bill Wilson and Larry Ames.

CHAPTER 8

Eich, Ritch K. "Remembering leaders who put country above party." *The Hill*, October 12, 2019.

CHAPTER 9

Zenger, Jack and Joseph Folkman. "Research: Women Score Higher Than Men in Most Leadership Skills." *Harvard Business Review*, June 25, 2019. https://hbr.org/2019/06/research-women-score-higher-than-men-in-most-leadership-skills

CHAPTER 11

https://www.radicati.com/?p=16516

https://www.statista.com/statistics/278414/number-of-worldwide-social-network-users/

https://simpletexting.com/all-the-text-marketing-statistics-you-need-to-know/

https://archive.org/details/@archiveofannualreports

https://behavioralvalueinvestor.com/blog/2018/6/14/5-exemplary-ceo-annual-letters-worth-reading

https://hbr.org/2011/02/secrets-of-positive-feedback

https://investorplace.com/2018/03/7-ceos-honest-with-shareholders/

https://thechickenwire.chick-fil-a.com/lifestyle/humble-at-the-top-why-these-ceos-still-write-thank-you-notes

https://www.businessinsider.com/ceo-writes-7400-employee-birthday-cards-each-year-2017-6

https://www.fastcompany.com/3035830/how-campbells-soups-former-ceo-turned-the-company-around

https://www.forbes.com/sites/laurarittenhouse/2019/12/10/find-ceo-brilliance-in-shareholder-letters/#2e0b3af336b8

https://www.forbes.com/sites/rodgerdeanduncan/2018/04/06/close-encounters-leadership-and-handwritten-notes/#29fea0483e96

https://www.inc.com/elisa-boxer/home-depots-ceo-did-this-25000-times-science-says-you-should-do-it-too.html

https://www.lawyersmutualnc.com/blog/how-thank-you-notes-saved-a-dying-company

https://www.preachingtoday.com/illustrations/2018/november/
famous-ceos-who-write-personal-thank-you-notes.html

https://www.quantifiedcommunications.com/blog/lets-be-
clear.-in-annual-shareholder-letters-how-can-ceos-make-
themselves-understood

https://www.simplemost.com/this-ceo-writes-9200-employee-
birthday-cards-a-year/

https://www.washingtonpost.com/lifestyle/how-george-
hw-bush-used-handwritten-thank-you-notes-to-ink-his-
values/2018/12/01/3f78a0b4-f59f-11e8-9240-e8028a62c722_
story.html

https://www.washingtonpost.com/news/on-leadership/
wp/2014/02/05/a-thank-you-note-from-mark-zuckerberg/

CHAPTER 12

https://www.pbs.org/newshour/show/why-pandemic-
represents-existential-crisis-for-performing-artists

INDEX

ABOUT THE AUTHOR

Ritch K. Eich PhD is a business leader, military officer, author, and tireless volunteer whose expertise on leadership has been recognized by many of America's top leaders in both the private and public sectors.

A fourth generation Californian who worked in the peach orchards of Yuba and Sutter counties every summer from his preteen years through college, Dr. Eich enlisted in the United States Naval Reserve while a senior at Sacramento State College. At Sacramento State, he was a letterman on the Far Western Conference Championship tennis team, served as vice president of the student body and was named District "Man of the Year" for the Sigma Phi Epsilon fraternity. He received the Associated Students "Distinguished Student Leader" award when he graduated.

Eich retired as a Navy captain after serving over twenty-nine years and receiving several commendations and medals including a Meritorious Mast from the Commanding Officer of Marine Barracks and the Navy's Meritorious Service Medal. The U.S. Naval Academy recognized Dr. Eich for his many years of service as a Blue and Gold Officer, recruiting outstanding young men and women to attend the service academy in Annapolis.

In addition to Sacramento State College, Dr. Eich is a graduate of Michigan State University, and the University of Michigan, where he received his PhD.

Dr. Eich has enjoyed a successful civilian career in several industries including healthcare, public relations, and higher education. He has served on more than a dozen boards of directors and trustees and facilitated the first multiyear corporate sponsorship between Blue Shield of California and the San Francisco Giants Baseball Club, to promote the prevention of domestic violence. He established the Corporate Leaders Breakfast/Speaker Series in Ventura County and was the first person to create parity for California Lutheran University's men's and women's athletic teams' identity and logotypes (Kingsmen and Regals), helping to bring equality to campus athletics.

Dr. Eich has also been an adjunct faculty member at several universities teaching courses in leadership, marketing, strategy, and organizational behavior and communication.

The author of four other books on leadership, Dr. Eich has donated all of the proceeds from sales of his books to the following charities:

Real Leaders Don't Boss: nonprofit organizations caring for military men and women wounded in Iraq or Afghanistan;

Leadership Requires Extra Innings: the Jackie Robinson Foundation for minority scholarships;

Truth, Trust + Tenacity: children's hospitals and the Ronald McDonald House; and

Leadership CPR: the nonprofit National Fallen Firefighters Foundation that honors firefighters killed in the line of duty and provides important help to their survivors so they can rebuild their lives; and to Concerns of Police Survivors, a nonprofit organization committed to rebuilding shattered lives through its services and programs.

Dr. Eich has contributed to local and national publications and news outlets including Bloomberg Business, *Forbes*, Fast Company, Investors Business Daily, *The Globe and Mail*, Directors & Boards, Fox News, *CEO Magazine*, Monster.com, Leadership Excellence (HR.com), *The Journal of Values-Based Leadership*, *The Hill*, Modern Healthcare, and many others.

He was the first naval reservist to lend his fundraising expertise to the founding president of the Washington, D.C.-based U.S. Navy Memorial to raise construction funds and an endowment.

Together with his wife, Joan, Dr. Eich established a scholarship program at Leadership San Francisco for applicants with financial need and was the first to establish a trustee scholarship at the University of California, Merced where he served as a founding trustee on the university's foundation board, and where he is now a Fellow.

The Eichs have volunteered for many civic organizations including United Way, March of Dimes, Farm and Garden, Crossroads Rehabilitation, and the Boys and Girls Scouts. For the past two decades, they have also served as volunteer marshals at more than a dozen major PGA Tour stops. The charitable proceeds from these golf tournaments benefit not-for-profit organizations in communities across the United States.

Ritch and Joan have two sons and daughters-in-law and four grandchildren. Dr. Eich can be contacted at ritcheich@gmail.com.